First World War
and Army of Occupation
War Diary
France, Belgium and Germany

60 DIVISION
Headquarters, Branches and Services
Royal Army Ordnance Corps
Deputy Assistant Director Ordnance Services
23 June 1916 - 31 October 1916

WO95/3026/10

The Naval & Military Press Ltd
www.nmarchive.com
Published in association with The National Archives

Published by

The Naval & Military Press Ltd

Unit 10 Ridgewood Industrial Park,

Uckfield, East Sussex,

TN22 5QE England

Tel: +44 (0) 1825 749494

www.naval-military-press.com

www.nmarchive.com

This diary has been reprinted in facsimile from the original. Any imperfections are inevitably reproduced and the quality may fall short of modern type and cartographic standards.

© **Crown Copyright**
Images reproduced by permission of The National Archives, London, England, 2015.

Contents

Document type	Place/Title	Date From	Date To
Heading	WO95/3026/10		
Heading	60th Division D.A. Dir Ordnance Services Jun-Oct 1916		
Heading	War Diary of Lieut E Watmough Army Ordnance Department D.A.D.O.S. 60th Division From 20th June 1916 To 30th June 1916 (Volume I)		
War Diary	France		
War Diary	Flers	23/06/1916	26/06/1916
War Diary	Villiers Chattel	27/06/1916	30/06/1916
Heading	War Diary of Lieut E Watmough Army Ordnance Department D.A.D.O.S. 60th Division From 1st July 1916 To 31st July 1916 Vol II		
War Diary	Villiers Chattel	01/07/1916	10/07/1916
War Diary	Hermaville	14/07/1916	31/07/1916
Heading	War Diary of Lieut E Watmough Army Ordnance Department D.A.D.O.S. 60th Division From 1.8.16 To 31.8.16 (Volume III)		
War Diary	Hermaville	01/08/1916	31/08/1916
Heading	War Diary of Lieut E. Watmough Army Ordnance Department D.A.D.O.S. 60th Division From 1.9.16 30.9.16 (Volume IV)		
War Diary	Hermaville	01/09/1916	30/09/1916
Heading	War Diary of Lieut E Watmough Army Ordnance Department D.A.D.O.S. 60th Lon Divn From October 1st 1916 To October 31st 1916 Volume V		
War Diary	Hermaville	01/10/1916	24/10/1916
War Diary	Houvin-Houvigneul	27/10/1916	28/10/1916
War Diary	Frohen-Le Grand	29/10/1916	29/10/1916
War Diary	Bernaville	30/10/1916	31/10/1916

WO 95/3026/10

60TH DIVISION

D.A.DIR ORDNANCE SERVICES
JUN - OCT 1916

CONFIDENTIAL

WAR DIARY

OF

Lieut: E. Watmough, Army Ordnance Department.
D.a.D.O.S. 60th Division.

(Volume 1)

From:- 20th June 1916.
To:- 30th June 1916.

WAR DIARY
or
INTELLIGENCE SUMMARY.
(Erase heading not required.)

Army Form C. 2118.

Instructions regarding War Diaries and Intelligence Summaries are contained in F. S. Regs., Part II. and the Staff Manual respectively. Title pages will be prepared in manuscript.

Hour, Date, Place		Summary of Events and Information	Remarks and references to Appendices
	FRANCE	Sailed arrived at BOULOGNE on arrival and motored from BOULOGNE to AUBIGNY where I stayed five days.	f/w
23.6.16.	FLERS	Left AUBIGNY and arrived at FLERS same day. Divisional Head Quarters at FLERS.	f/w
22.6.16.	FLERS	Submitted indents to HAVRE for stores which were authorised for issue in FRANCE but not authorised for issue under mobilization Store Tables G 1098 Series.	f/w
25.6.16.	"	My Staff, consisting of 1 Lt. Ordnance Officer, Non-commissioned and men arrived at FLERS.	f/w
26.6.16.	"	Three lorries were allotted to me on this date. Consignments of 1900 Shelmets C.H. for Divisional Reserve arrived.	f/w
27.6.16.	VILLIERS CHATTEL	Moved to VILLIERS CHATTEL, and established Office.	f/w
29.6.16.	"	First consignment of steel Shelmets received (7000). Issue made immediately.	f/w
30.6.16.	"	Fifty two Lewis machine guns complete received. These were issued to Lining Battalions up to a total strength of 8 each.	f/w

Vol II

CONFIDENTIAL

WAR DIARY

OF

Lieut: E. Waimough. Army Ordnance Department.
D.A.D.O.S. 60th Division.

(Volume 2).

From: 1st July 1916.　　　　　　　　To: 31st July 1916.

Army Form C. 2118.

WAR DIARY
or
INTELLIGENCE SUMMARY.
(Erase heading not required.)

Instructions regarding War Diaries and Intelligence Summaries are contained in F. S. Regs., Part II. and the Staff Manual respectively. Title pages will be prepared in manuscript.

Hour, Date, Place	Summary of Events and Information	Remarks and references to Appendices
1.7.16 TOWERS CHAMBER	Commenced new System of Stock Issues i.e.: Demanding a from quantity of Ordnance Stores in Bulk, certain stores being demanded in Bulk each day. This system will often already amount of stores issued. date of such issue. The Units indent No: and date such a reference to the units receipt of such stores. Divisional Baths started. Most Ordnance armourers and smiths busy N.C.O. and men of 7th Division to have a bath. ce: about 1000 a week. Indents submitted for 1000 pairs Socks, 1000 Shirts, 750 Drawers cotton, and 250 Drawers Woollen for Pime Baths.	Su
3.7.16 " "	Stores received from Base. Wikibillers to work made. Standard for Stores Mortars received.	Su
4.7.16 " "	HQ80 Sringa Brow lorries arrived, also 1550 Blankets, Blankets issued at rate of 2.5% strength of Formations. 2,080 magazines for Lewis machine guns arrived.	Su
5.7.16 " "	Divisional Workshops started. Armourers. Bootmakers Sailors.	Su
6.7.16 " "	Various stores received from Base.	

(9 29 6) W 2791 100,000 8/14 H W V   Forms/C. 2118/11.

WAR DIARY or INTELLIGENCE SUMMARY.

(Erase heading not required.)

Army Form C. 2118.

Instructions regarding War Diaries and Intelligence Summaries are contained in F. S. Regs., Part II. and the Staff Manual respectively. Title pages will be prepared in manuscript.

Hour, Date, Place	Summary of Events and Information	Remarks and references to Appendices
7.7.16 VILLIERS CHATEL	Various stores received including 100 Periscopes, 51000 Safety Pins for use with Anti-gas Helmets, 2200 Bone Respirators. Army Order received authorizing the issue of Gas Brass to approved Officers N.C.O.'s and men.	
8.7.16 " " "	288 Kinds of stores received from Rone. Distribution to units made.	
10.7.16 " " "	Showering Stitcher arrived from 2/15 Bn London Regt to replace one destroyed by Shell fire. Large quantity of stores received from Rone.	
14. HERMAVILLE	Moved to HERMAVILLE. This move took approximately four hours. Ex Minimum Reserve of 19,040 Steel Helmets moved from VILLIERS CHATEL to HERMAVILLE. Received four dumps for stores, one for 179th Brigade, 180, one for 181st and one for Reserve Dumps. Buzzer Wire despatched for Book, Equipment, see Funds of Oil and Grease, Soap and Thrum Shoes, the Bulk wire was consolidated. Demand for requirements of the whole of the 60th Division.	
15th " " "	3,294 Steel Helmets received and distributed. Various other stores received.	

Army Form C. 2118.

WAR DIARY
or
INTELLIGENCE SUMMARY.
(Erase heading not required.)

Instructions regarding War Diaries and Intelligence Summaries are contained in F. S. Regs., Part II. and the Staff Manual respectively. Title pages will be prepared in manuscript.

Hour, Date, Place	Summary of Events and Information	Remarks and references to Appendices
16.7.16 HERMAVILLE	Stores received from Cars and distributed. Distribution of stores is made every day. All units calling and taking them away. General Wires Road to be sent tomorrow morning to call and collect their stores.	
17.7.16 " "	Large quantities of stores received from Cars and distributed. Commenced rendering a report to D.A.Q.M.G. 100th Division shewing all important stores received up to 7 p.m. daily. This report is to be rendered by 7 p.m. every day.	
18.7.16 " "	All kinds of stores received from Cars, including 8½ miles of Electric Cable and 104 Snipescopes and 48 Stove-pipe attachments for the same and Vickers Guns. 353 Box Respirators received and distributed to Infantry.	
19.7.16 " "	1000 Steel Helmets received and distributed. 80 Shields for protection of Bombers received & also large quantity of stores. One Vickers machine demanded to replace one damaged by rifle fire. Large quantity of stores received.	

Army Form C. 2118.

WAR DIARY
or
INTELLIGENCE SUMMARY.
(Erase heading not required.)

Instructions regarding War Diaries and Intelligence Summaries are contained in F. S. Regs., Part II. and the Staff Manual respectively. Title pages will be prepared in manuscript.

Hour, Date, Place	Summary of Events and Information	Remarks and references to Appendices
20.7.16 HERMAVILLE	Large quantity of stores received and distributed. One Vickers Gun received for 181st Machine Gun Company.	
21.7.16 " "	Stores received from Base and distributed.	
22.7.16 " "	Indents submitted to HAVRE for 500 Smoke Helmets. Stores received from Base and distributed. All demands for stores to be sent to Calais instead of Havre.	
23.7.16 " "	Stores received from Base and distributed.	
24.7.16 " "	Stores received and distributed.	
25.9.16 " "	Clothing and various stores received and distributed.	
26.7.16 " "	500 Smoke Helmets received and other stores.	
27.7.16 " "	Stores received from Base and distributed.	
28.7.16 " "	Large quantity of stores received from Base, including 72 Rifles, Signal, 290 Pistols Smith & Wesson.	
30.9.16 " "	14+20 Slitmili Anti-gas received, 1400 Steel Helmets, 246 Carriers Magazine and various other small stores.	
31.7.16 " "	392 Carriers Magazine received, 2.40 Sheets for protection of Ambuses and all kinds of other stores.	

CONFIDENTIAL

WAR DIARY

OF

Lieut: E. Watmough. Army Ordnance Department
D.A.D.O.S. 60th Division.

From: 1.8.16.   To: 31.8.16.

(Volume VII).

Army Form C. 2118.

WAR DIARY
or
INTELLIGENCE SUMMARY.
(Erase heading not required.)

Instructions regarding War Diaries and Intelligence Summaries are contained in F. S. Regs., Part II. and the Staff Manual respectively. Title pages will be prepared in manuscript.

Hour, Date, Place	Summary of Events and Information	Remarks and references to Appendices
1.8.16. HERMAVILLE	Quantity of stores received from base and distributed.	
2.8.16.	Stores received from base.	
3.8.16.	Indents submitted to Base for 2 (B) & 13 pdr 9 cwt guns for HQ anti-aircraft Battery. Stores received from Base and distributed.	
5.8.16.	Indents submitted for one three inch Stokes Smoke mortar to replace one destroyed by shell fire. 300 Steel Shelmets received.	
6.8.16.	631 Steel Shelmets received and issued. Various other stores received.	
7.8.16.	2 – 18 pounder carriages fitted with Aut. receiver gears received, and 300 13 pounder 9 cwt guns received for HQ Anti-Aircraft Battery by lorry from Calais.	
8.8.16.	300 magazines for Lewis Guns received, and various other stores.	
9.8.16.	552 Ground Sheeting received. 5 #50 Box Shelmets and other stores.	
10.8.16.	Stores received from base and distributed.	
11.8.16.	50 machinegun Sprayers received and other stores.	
12.8.16.	Indents submitted for one Lewis Machine Gun to replace one destroyed by shell fire, for 2/23rd Bn Imam Regt.	

Army Form C. 2118.

WAR DIARY
or
INTELLIGENCE SUMMARY.
(Erase heading not required.)

Instructions regarding War Diaries and Intelligence Summaries are contained in F. S. Regs., Part II. and the Staff Manual respectively. Title pages will be prepared in manuscript.

Hour, Date, Place	Summary of Events and Information	Remarks and references to Appendices
13.8.16. HERMAVILLE.	Large quantity of stores received. Proceeded to AMIENS to purchase stores, including kit for making Signposts for Engineers to Aerodrome.	
14.8.16. "	2250 Gas Helmets received and all Stores of other sorts.	
15.8.16. "	One Lewis machine Gun received for 2/23rd Bn London Regt. Proceeded to St POL to purchase stores.	
16.8.16. "	One Wagon G.S. received. Also 1410 Gas Helmets, 4 Shields for machine Gunners, and various other smoke stores.	
18.8.16 "	150 Steel Helmets received and various.	
19.8.16 "	One Vickers Machine Gun received for 1817 machine Gun Company	
20.8.16 "	Large quantity of stores received from store including 750 Steel Helmets.	
21.8.16 "	Large quantity of stores received from store.	
22.8.16 "	85 Buzzers received for Artillery. Proceeded to St POL to purchase stores. Remained on 18 pdr Gun fire Battery 300" hole.	
23.8.16 "	850 Steel Helmets received and a large quantity of other stores.	

WAR DIARY
or
INTELLIGENCE SUMMARY.
(Erase heading not required.)

Army Form C. 2118.

Instructions regarding War Diaries and Intelligence Summaries are contained in F. S. Regs., Part II. and the Staff Manual respectively. Title pages will be prepared in manuscript.

Hour, Date, Place	Summary of Events and Information	Remarks and references to Appendices
24.8.16 HERMAVILLE	One ordnance S.A.A. 18p. rounder Gun received for 'C' Battery	
	300" fuzes R.A. to replace one burst near muzzle. Present submitted for one complete Barrel casing for Vickers Gun for 180th Machine Gun Company to replace damaged by three fire. Base wires saying complete.	
	9p Barrel casing not received, and order passed for new Gun.	
25.8.16 - " -	Breech fittings and carriage complete received for 'C' Battery 300" Brigade R.T.A. Large quantity of other stores	
	9p received.	
26.8.16 - " -	2517 Magazines for Lewis Gun received and distributed. Large quantity of other stores received. Demanded one Stand for 3 inch Stokes Howitzer to replace damaged by Shell	
	3 fire.	
27.8.16 - " -	Received one Vickers machine Gun for 180th Machine Gun	
	9p Company. Quantity of other stores received.	
28.8.16 - " -	9p Satchels received for anti-gas shelmets. (4691).	

WAR DIARY or INTELLIGENCE SUMMARY.

Army Form C. 2118.

(Erase heading not required.)

Instructions regarding War Diaries and Intelligence Summaries are contained in F. S. Regs., Part II. and the Staff Manual respectively. Title pages will be prepared in manuscript.

Hour, Date, Place	Summary of Events and Information	Remarks and references to Appendices
28.8.16 HERMAVILLE	Indent submitted for one H.S. inch "Howitzer for D Battery 303rd Brigade R.F.A. to replace one damaged by explosion in chamber. Proceeded to AMIENS to purchase stores.	
29.8.16 " "	Indent submitted for one Lewis machine gun for 2/16th Bn London Regt to replace one destroyed by shell fire. Indent submitted for 3 inch mortar and spare parts for 180th Bde to replace one destroyed by shell fire. Large quantity of stores received from Base. Allowed conference on the Question of stores received from Base.	
30.8.16 " "	Drawing of stores received from Base. One H.S. Howitzer received for D Battery 303rd Brigade R.F.A. Proceeded to PREVENT to intervene Supplies of Ordnance machinery. Heavy mobile Workshops. Store received from Base and distributed.	

Vol 4

CONFIDENTIAL

WAR DIARY

OF

Lieut. E. Watmough. Army Ordnance Department. D.a.D.O.S. 60th Division.

From: 1.9.1916   30.9.1916.

(Volume IV).

WAR DIARY or INTELLIGENCE SUMMARY

(Erase heading not required.)

Army Form C. 2118.

Hour, Date, Place	Summary of Events and Information	Remarks and references to Appendices
1.9.16. HERMAVILLE	Visited 2/5" and 2/6" Field Ambulances and inspected Divisional Stores. 72 Handcarts for Lewis Machine Guns received and large quantity of other stores.	
2.9.16 " " "	Bossceed adaptors from Seavey Mobile Workshops, FREVENT. Steel Helmets received from Base. Demands submitted to Base for accessories for Lewis Handcarts, Sniper Veils and Dummy cartridges.	
3.9.16 " " "	Sent to Ordnance Workshops, FREVENT in connection with Breech Mechanisms. Two Stokes Gun arrived for 1/4" Battn. Germany. Stores received from Base.	
4.9.16 " " "	Went to St POL by motor to purchase stores. Went from ST POL to FREVENT and handed over 28 pairs of Rifle Barrels to Armourer who connecting pieces for the Emplacement.	
5.9.16 " " "	Sent to FREVENT with Lewis Gun Magazines for alteration. 18 pdr Gun reported damaged, but repaired by I.O.M.	
6.9.16 " " "	Visited 2/4" Field Ambulance and inspected Divisional...	

Army Form C. 2118.

WAR DIARY
or
INTELLIGENCE SUMMARY.
(Erase heading not required.)

Instructions regarding War Diaries and Intelligence Summaries are contained in F. S. Regs., Part II. and the Staff Manual respectively. Title pages will be prepared in manuscript.

Hour, Date, Place	Summary of Events and Information	Remarks and references to Appendices
6.9.16. HERMAVILLE	Stores. Inspected all Battalion Quartermaster stores with Staff Captain of 179th Infantry Bde, including machine gun Company transports of 179th Bde Stores and all outstanding indents Rectified.	
7.9.16 " "	Inspection of ammunition returns to improve Levil Workshops and to visit all ammunition in the Divisions. Sent to St POL to purchase various stores.	
8.9.16 " "	Visited 180th Battery from 2nd Reserve, also 2/17, 2/18, 2/19, 2/20 Battalions, London Regt and machine Gun Bn and found all Quartermaster stores in good order. Inspection of Ammunition wanted all ammunition in 180th Infantry Bde. Ammunition Staff Sergeant returned from Steavy mobile Workshops. Twenty Lee Enfield attachments sent in for repair. Four MC were made in ten minutes.	
9.9.16 " "	Inspection of Ammunition took Telescopic Rifle 15 Avrs. La Chateau. Rifle could not be repaired. Collected aeroplane pieces for attachments	

Army Form C. 2118.

WAR DIARY
or
INTELLIGENCE SUMMARY.
(Erase heading not required.)

Instructions regarding War Diaries and Intelligence Summaries are contained in F. S. Regs., Part II. and the Staff Manual respectively. Title pages will be prepared in manuscript.

Hour, Date, Place	Summary of Events and Information	Remarks and references to Appendices
9.9.16 HERMAVILLE	On 2" Trench Mortars.	
10.9.16 " "	Inspector of Armourers went by car to 179th Infantry Brigade to inspect armourer. 2" Trench Mortar in Y.bi Trench Mortar battery damaged, and condemned by 10 a.m. New one issued. Jn. visited Divisional Shoe Repairers with reference to local purchases. Came under 1st Army at 12 noon.	
11.9.16 " "	Inspector of Armourers completed work with 1st Division. 80 No. 9 periscopes received and large quantity of existing ones can be damaged at AMIENS. Went received saying returning next day.	
12.9.16 " "	Attended conference at Divisional Shoe Repairers with detail. Explain large quantity of stores received.	
13.9.16 " "	Car still under repair. Westspring Jun received from a DOS XVIIth Corps. Quantity of shirts received from base including 100 steel shell nets and 500 blankets.	
14.9.16 " "	Car returned. Large quantity of stores received from base.	
15.9.16 " "	Emergency issue for whole Lotterchene including gas helmets.	

Army Form C. 2118.

WAR DIARY
or
INTELLIGENCE SUMMARY.
(Erase heading not required.)

Instructions regarding War Diaries and Intelligence Summaries are contained in F. S. Regs., Part II. and the Staff Manual respectively. Title pages will be prepared in manuscript.

Hour, Date, Place	Summary of Events and Information	Remarks and references to Appendices
15.9.16 HERMAVILLE	Two 9.15" Mortars collected from workshops Bury and taken to MAROEUIL by lorry. Lorry sent to FREVENT with scrap metal etc.	
16.9.16	Visited Divisional Head Quarters. Visited 'C' & 'B' Batteries of 30th Brigade R.F.A. and 'A', 'B' and 'C' Batteries of 302nd Brigade R.F.A.	
17.9.16	Visited Divisional Head Quarters. a large quantity of stores received from base.	
18.9.16	Visited ST POL and made various purchases. Gun parts received from Base. Leather and Bindery picketing gear and various other stores.	
19.9.16	Attended Conference at Divisional Head Quarters at 2.0.p.m. Army made an inspection of Supt. Jelmes C.S.I. and B.A.U. received from Base. Stopcocks, Gun parts and all kinds of other stores.	
20.9.16	Visited Quartermaster Stores of Battalion of 18th Infantry Bde. 1100 pairs of Boots F.S. received. 1008 pairs Gum Boots and	

(9) 26 (9) W 7624 100,000 5/15 H W V Forms C. 2118/11.

WAR DIARY
or
INTELLIGENCE SUMMARY.

(Erase heading not required.)

Army Form C. 2118.

Instructions regarding War Diaries and Intelligence Summaries are contained in F. S. Regs., Part II. and the Staff Manual respectively. Title pages will be prepared in manuscript.

Hour, Date, Place	Summary of Events and Information	Remarks and references to Appendices
20.9.16 HERMAVILLE	300 Blankets also received.	
21.9.16 " " "	Visited Divisional Head Quarters. Inspector of Armourers left for Buly with VII Corps Service. Officer Armourers inspected Workshop. Large quantity of stores received from there.	
22.9.16 " " "	Visited all Arty. units. 2/6 and 2/5 field Ambulances. "D" Battery 301st Bde. "D" Battery 302nd Bde. and a. B.C. & D. Batteries 303rd Brigade. Lewis Gun Parts and Blankets received from them.	
23.9.16 " " "	Visited ST POL and made various purchases. 300 Breech Covers received from there, and Rifle Covers, Blankets Periscopes and various other small items.	
24.9.16 " " "	Quartermasters in from units to check indents. One forward to Corps. Established new dump owing to the Large numbers of Blankets received from there.	
25.9.16 " " "	Visited Snipers School with Inspector telescope Rifle Sights Gun condemned by I.O.M. and new ones demanded from Pank.	

Forms/C. 2118/11.

WAR DIARY or INTELLIGENCE SUMMARY.

(Erase heading not required.)

Army Form C. 2118.

Instructions regarding War Diaries and Intelligence Summaries are contained in F. S. Regs., Part II. and the Staff Manual respectively. Title pages will be prepared in manuscript.

Hour, Date, Place	Summary of Events and Information	Remarks and references to Appendices
25.9.16 HERMAVILLE	288 Rounds of practising gun ammunition from France and quantity of other stores.	
26.9.16 " " "	Visited A.D.C. units 180th Infantry Bde. and R.E. stores. 11 men found for training in Divisional Workshop. Lorry collection mountings from 1st Army R.E. Workshop. 9 + 3 Stoke Helmets and large quantity of other stores received.	
27.9.16 " " "	Lorry collected Rifle Grenade Stands from 1st Army Workshop and 2" Trench Mortars from 8th Division. Quantity of stores received from France.	
28.9.16 " " "	Visited AMIENS and made various purchases including drawing materials for Taylors Shop 2 two inch and 1 Three inch French Strinkers received from France	
29.9.16 " " "	Visited a D.O.S. XVIIth Corps and Heen Cartier. Large quantity of stores received from France.	
30.9.16 " " "	One 2" Trench mortar reported out of action. Quantity of stores received from containing 2 Harvesto of Dumps.	

Vol 5

CONFIDENTIAL

WAR DIARY

of

Lieut E Watrough, Army Ordnance Department
D.ADOS. 1st Cav. Divn.

From October 1st 1916   To October 31st 1916

Volume V

Army Form C. 2118.

WAR DIARY
INTELLIGENCE SUMMARY.
(Erase heading not required.)

Instructions regarding War Diaries and Intelligence Summaries are contained in F. S. Regs., Part II. and the Staff Manual respectively. Title pages will be prepared in manuscript.

Hour, Date, Place	Summary of Events and Information	Remarks and references to Appendices
1-10-16. HERMAVILLE	Car lent to S.O.M. SAVY to proceed to BETHUNE. Two French mortars reported out of action but repairable. Lorry lent to E.R.O. to convey three 2" mortars from MAROEUIL to French Mortar School.	
2-10-16 "	General office routine. No stores arrived from base.	
3-10-16 "	A.D.O.S. XVII Corps called during the afternoon. Owing to no stores arriving on previous day, a double load of stores were received today	
5-10-16 "	Visited 2/1st 2/5th 2/6th Field Ambulances, and found all stores in good order. Inspected four repairing shops. Full quantity of Leather has not come up from Base, thereby causing some delay in repairing boots. Two 2" and One 3" mortars repaired and returned today. Sent one lorry load of metal to FREVENT. One lorry took 2" French Mortar to MAROEUIL	
6-10-16 "	Visited A.D.O.S and S.O.M. SAVY with reference to French mortars	

Army Form C. 2118.

WAR DIARY
or
INTELLIGENCE SUMMARY.
(Erase heading not required.)

Instructions regarding War Diaries and Intelligence Summaries are contained in F. S. Regs., Part II. and the Staff Manual respectively. Title pages will be prepared in manuscript.

Hour, Date, Place		Summary of Events and Information	Remarks and references to Appendices
6-10-16 (cont.)	HERMAVILLE.	Inspected D.A.C. Q.M. Stores & found everything in good order and no surplus stores.	
		4.5" How. reported out of action owing to premature in bore.	
7-10-16	"	Lorry sent to S.O.M. SAVY.	
		Machine gun of 181st M.G. Coy out of action and sent to I.O.M. SAVY.	
8-10-16	"	Sent car with 2" Trench Mortar to No. 8 Workshop.	
		500 additional Gum boots issued to each Infantry Brigade and 100 to Pioneer Battalion.	
9-10-16	"	Visited 179th Inf. Bde (all units) including Machine Gun Coy. and inspected all Q.M. stores and found everything in good order, no surplus stores. Also visited R.O.O. Railhead re special rack of clothing.	
		A.D.O.S. called during afternoon.	

Army Form C. 2118.

WAR DIARY
or
INTELLIGENCE SUMMARY.
(Erase heading not required.)

Instructions regarding War Diaries and Intelligence Summaries are contained in F. S. Regs., Part II. and the Staff Manual respectively. Title pages will be prepared in manuscript.

Hour, Date, Place	Summary of Events and Information	Remarks and references to Appendices
10-10-16. HERMAVILLE	Visited all units of 180th Brigade with A.D.V.S. XVII Corps. All stores were found to be in good order and no surplus. 3 Forges arrived from AMIENS which had been purchased. Six Stoves Soyers received from Corps to complete the Division to 60.	
11-10-16 "	1250 Lamps Hurricane drawn from Railhead for Division. A.D.V.S. called during afternoon. Fire practice carried out.	
12-10-16 "	Visited A.S.C. (all units) in the morning. All stores found in good order. One 2" French Mortar destroyed. 4.5" Howitzer arrived.	
13-10-16 "	Went to AMIENS and purchased six chaff cutters together with various other items. Also paid for forges. 3" French Mortar kit direct and condemned by F.O.M.	
14-10-16. "	Visited 181 Infantry Brigade and 181 M.G. Coy., all stores found correct and in good order. Second Blankets issued to units in the back area.	

Army Form C. 2118.

WAR DIARY
or
INTELLIGENCE SUMMARY

(*Erase heading not required.*)

Instructions regarding War Diaries and Intelligence Summaries are contained in F. S. Regs., Part II. and the Staff Manual respectively. Title Pages will be prepared in manuscript.

Place	Date	Hour	Summary of Events and Information	Remarks and references to Appendices
HERMAVILLE	15-10-16	—	Visited Divisional Headquarters. Train arrived very late with stores owing to trucks being sent to FREVENT-CAPELLE instead of AUBIGNY. Large quantity of serviceable and unserviceable stores sent to Base. 4000 Expes. Machinets arrived.	
"	16-10-16	—	Attended conference at Divisional Headquarters. Car in dock for overhaul. 3" Stokes Gun arrived.	
"	17-10-16	—	Visited S. O. M. SAVY, A.S.O.S. XVII Corps and Railhead. Stores for Artillery and other units brought from SAVY by lorry. One lorry load of old metal sent to Heavy Mobile Workshops. FREVENT.	
"	19-10-16	—	Visited DADOS 24th Division. General office routine.	
"	20-10-16	—	Visited D.A.E. and Field Ambulances. All stores in good condition & no surplus. DADOS 3rd Canadian Division visited dumps and arranged taking over. Sent lorry to BETHUNE to collect rifle meat. Group re-divided. Field Service Boots arrived. Visited Supply Column re lorries.	
"	21-10-16	—	Clearing up surplus & eye stores and making arrangements for move generally.	
"	22-10-16	—	Visited A.S.O.S. XVII Corps. 3rd Canadian Ordnance arrived. Distributed Boots F.S. Visited Divisional Headquarters re move. No train arrived with stores.	
"	23-10-16	—	Went to CAUROY to inspect new place for dumps, but all arrangements were cancelled at night. Car broke spring coming back and went to Column for repair. Wired to Base to suspend all issues owing to impending move.	

Army Form C. 2118.

WAR DIARY
or
INTELLIGENCE SUMMARY

(Erase heading not required.)

Instructions regarding War Diaries and Intelligence Summaries are contained in F. S. Regs., Part II. and the Staff Manual respectively. Title Pages will be prepared in manuscript.

Place	Date	Hour	Summary of Events and Information	Remarks and references to Appendices
HERMAVILLE	24-10-16	—	Car taken away and pooled. Units all on the move which made it very difficult to distribute stores. Base sent up a very large amount of stores. Also called during afternoon and had an interview with D.A.D.O.S. 3rd Can. Divn.	
"	25-10-16	—	Clearing dumps and handing over stores to D.A.D.O.S. 3rd Canadian Divn. Also transferred all artillery B.A.R. No 1 Sec. 21st Res. Pk. No 1 Co. A.S.C. etc. to Canadian Division.	
"	26-10-16	—	Moved from HERMAVILLE to HOUVIN-HOUVIGNEUL via AVNES-LE-COMTE and ETRÉE-WAMIN. Moved in two journeys. Left Salvage Corps men to deal with surplus & r/s stores.	
HOUVIN-HOUVIGNEUL	27-10-16	—	Sent lorries to respective Brigades with stores. Went to FREVENT to try and purchase cloth for making distinguishing badges, but could not get any.	
"	28-10-16	—	Moved from HOUVIN-HOUVIGNEUL to FROHEN-LE-GRAND via FREVENT, BOURQUEMAISON, BARLY and MÉZEROLLES. One lorry returned to clear balance of stores.	
FROHEN-LE-GRAND	29-10-16	—	Moved from FROHEN-LE-GRAND to BERNAVILLE via MÉZEROLLES and LE MEILLARD. Cleared all stores in four lorries in convoy. Arrived at BERNAVILLE at 10-45 A.M. and proceeded to open dumps.	
BERNAVILLE	30-10-16	—	Lorries sent to COMTEVILLE (on railhead) to collect fur coats but although advised by the R.T.O. that truck would be there by 9.15 pm, lorries had to go to FREVENT and did not return until 10-30 pm. Went to AMIENS to purchase cloth etc.	
"	31-10-16	—	Issued fur coats. Large quantity of r/s stores brought in by units.	